I HATE PARTIES

I HATE PARTIES

JES BATTIS

NIGHTWOOD EDITIONS
2024

1 2 3 4 5 — 28 27 26 25 24

Nightwood Editions
P.O. Box 1779
Gibsons, BC V0N 1V0
Canada
www.nightwoodeditions.com

COVER DESIGN: Angela Yen
COVER PHOTO: Devin Wilger
TYPOGRAPHY: Rafael Chimicatti

Nightwood Editions acknowledges the support of the Canada Council for the Arts, the Government of Canada, and the Province of British Columbia through the BC Arts Council.

This book has been printed on 100% post-consumer recycled paper.

Printed and bound in Canada.

LIBRARY AND ARCHIVES CANADA CATALOGUING IN PUBLICATION

Title: I hate parties / Jes Battis.
Other titles: I hate parties (Compilation)
Names: Battis, Jes, 1979- author.
Description: Poems.
Identifiers: Canadiana (print) 20240380886 | Canadiana (ebook) 20240384962 | ISBN 9780889714809 (softcover) | ISBN 9780889714786 (EPUB)
Subjects: LCGFT: Poetry.
Classification: LCC PS8603.A8785 I24 2024 | DDC C811/.6—dc23

I exist somewhere between the delivery
of chicken fingers and the taxi home

— MATTHEW WALSH,
"Driving by the Donkey Statue"

CONTENTS

3. Episodes

4. Transits

1. PENALTIES

Triple Axel

I pretend to be ill
so I can watch figure skating
at Lillehammer. It's 1994
and my mom and I are united
in our hatred of Elvis Stojko
whose quads feel empty
like a bear bluff-charging.

We watch Grinkov and Gordeeva
in seafoam velvet. She cleaves
to him, weightless, a single
cloud formation. When she skates
alone for the first time, after
his heart attack, their daughter
will pat her arm gently.

Though I dream of Paul Wylie's evangelical
ass in tights, I only have eyes
for Brian Boitano, queerly electric
in a pirate outfit
tearing through the long program
until he falls on the triple axel
combo shattered
our gasps
the floral quilt tossed aside
to peer closer at the screen.

Six years ago in Calgary
it was the Battle of the Brians
with Orser and Boitano dance-
fighting, one Brian in classic
black, the other in blue sequins,
two comets against the drab
orange arena. Shakespearean
rivalry of gays, those lines
of beauty, still closeted,
but couldn't I see it
even then?

This: the gayest thing to watch
in Chilliwack at the time. Both
Brians locked in combat. Galindo
screaming for joy at the US
Championship. Voice of Toller
Cranston in our ears, smooth
as fresh ice. They all dance
around me, skates winking fire,
gold trim, epaulettes, death
spiral of AIDS before
the cocktail. It spins us
still, and we are snow
under the blade.

I come out a year before Orser
glides to Neil Diamond. "The Story
of My Life." If I'd waited a year,
I might have ridden Ellen's
wave. I'm always
at the wrong party. Instead

it's Brian and Brian who push me
out of the stands. Those gods
in blue fire. Suspending
this long cold war

to spin me, once
again
and then
hurl me through space.

Sleepover

At thirteen, the gayest thing
you could do was sleep over
at a boy's house trying not to touch.
But you always did, fluttering, awkward,
marked by nervous laughter. Undressing
beneath his DC Talk posters
in carpeted rooms, or basements
where the air was lighter, cooler,
next to the pile of VHS tapes.

Those plastic covers squeaking
open as you drew out the title chosen
for nudity, loose jokes, actors
forgotten in films about sexy carwashes.
Like you, perhaps, they undressed
with wilder hopes. Odd tan lines,
stuffed briefs, legs white like bulk beans,
like your own, startled by touch.

You came accidentally, horribly,
in the hot tub. Begged to stay
while he towelled off. Cooking in
your shame as life crisped around
the edges. The whole night liquid
as you rolled on the waterbed.
What did you want, swimmer?
To kiss his freckled back? Or
to float in that sturdy frame,
wrinkling to a new texture?

Strip away everything, like
Eustace when the lion tears away
his dragon scales. All quiet on
the bunk bed. The tape clicking
to a stop. Don't look at him.
Not his high arches, not his armpits,
not his hair, not his mouth.

Look instead at the hummingbird decal
peeling off the window. A precaution
against birds who can't tell glass
from open air. Feel the boundary
against your skin. The red ache
of your wings.

Four-way Stop

I'm a four-way stop
in this red corduroy coat
when a seagull
perfectly spatters me
in white. I drift through
goal posts and walk along
the edge of blackberries
and confetti from dirty magazines.

I've got a meeting with some crows
who want to discuss projects.

You're a copper brush cut
with a dog named Shadow.
Your mom smokes constantly
and lets us watch *The Serpent
and the Rainbow*. Your dad
is a thin switchblade. His eyes
carve our initials. Mostly we're
alone in the house that smells
of hairspray. The dog growls
on the deck. I want to leave,
and also stay.

I can't remember meeting.
What did we say? Two little moons
on a collision course. Held back
for different reasons. You're
everyday dangerous, like
kitchen shears. I keep you
in my peripheral vision. But
you never hurt me. Your touch
is light, though not technically kind.

We ruin each other on a pile
of *Silver Surfer* comics. I see
the fear in your eyes as gravity
reverses. You stare at my empty
goldfish bowl where the cat
was recently sated. Now
we're both shadows
weathering the bed of rocks.

Bear of My Youth

I crossed the Port Mann bridge
to meet you, listening to Delirium
and the sound of my engine
failing.

You whipped out a Rainbow Brite
wallet in the food court. I was scared
by how brilliant you were, how
visible.

Your BFA project was melting
Barbie heads for credit. I failed
to ask proper questions about your
volcano.

We stayed on our safe sides of the
chesterfield. Your fun fur, every
part of you, inviting touch, but I
couldn't.

You adjusted your Vicki Gabereau
glasses, let me talk about Dippity
Do called *apeiron* holding life
together.

I wanted to kiss you and steal your
ideas. Wanted to melt, a changeling,
Barbie's painted eye, into what we actually
were.

What I'd say to you now, bear of my youth,
is, *You are perfect.* The hair visible through
your collar is perfect. The slope of your belly,
perfect.

Those days were bearish, warm, still half-
asleep, but I would have unseamed my pelt,
let you touch the truth and bright matter
underneath.

Little Earthquakes

In bed, we replay *Little Earthquakes*
searching for the Tori Amos song
that resonates with our drama.

We go out to eat, and I wonder
if you'll order both oysters
and snails, like Laurence Olivier
seducing Tony Curtis
in *Spartacus.* The waiter smirks
and you say, *He knows.*

You make my small town
nervous. In your silk shirt, I feel
your heart hammer beneath
the liquid blue. Your shy look
when I call you beautiful.

You breathe on my chest
to ease the eczema scars.
It's not working. My skin
holds the gauze touch
of your mouth.

You close the screen door
in my face, drawing a line
between the dark suburban street
and my weakness.

Foucault says putting your lover
in a taxi is the highest form
of desire. But at eighteen
I don't know shit,
barefoot on the front step,
feeling every earthquake.

Small-town Gays

Haunt the ice rink
sipping hot chocolate
trying not to think
about the curve
on his stick.

Confess everything
to eunuchs and dark elves
in fantasy novels
their lips cool
as a lick from a Dilly Bar
stolen in secret.

Dub it all
on mixtapes
that can't hold the sound
but capture
only
the hiss of geese
in our yards.

Watch his legs
pump the pedals
wondering
which laws of physics
must break
for us to touch
that hot element.

Double bounce
into orbit
animal satellites
knowing
the hard kiss
of the springs.

Camp and drink
bottles gleam
like votive candles
breath
on our cheek
unzip the sleeping bag
dive into dark waters.

Peel sunburnt skin
digging under pink
until we reach
the freon blue Slurpee
heart that we share.

Stand on the porch
raccoons caught
in misadventure
hands pressed together
as we wait
for our stippled kin
to hold
all of this.

I Hate Parties

Sweaty hand held inches from the door
and once again I check the mental map
of what you should and shouldn't do at parties
disintegrating ledger of names and faces
garden plot of twilight-blooming footnotes
long step inside, and everything goes blank.

The music scores my mind a perfect blank
as I line my shoes up cleanly by the door
now my socks resemble faded footnotes
lost in the hallway, searching for a map
I reach the warm room, dim and full of faces
remembering the shame of other parties.

Sometimes people are their own bright parties
a string of lights, but I'm the bulb left blank
squinting at the grammar of those swift faces
who will notice if I linger by the door
I fold and unfold, carefully, the map
tripping over shoes like fallen footnotes.

They're my favourite part, you say, *the footnotes*
but you would always come alive at parties
making risky turns without a map
being social was a kind of blank
cheque. You parachuted through the door
already pumping hands and making faces.

I say, *They're not my favourite part, the faces*
shifting on the page, unstable footnotes
things should stay the same: an orange, a door
that lets you leave interminable parties
your finger brushes mine, and all the blank
enclosures bloom, black ink spots on my map.

I find the kitchen, but I can't quite map
this night, your hand, the alphabet of faces
all my words are driftwood, bleached blank
by fear, and when I touch the older footnotes
they lead us down a cosmic line of parties
where you can run but never find the door,

and then your breath: *Let's use the secret door*
my favourite part is leaving all those parties
with you, cold air, warm cheek, hushed little footnotes.

Hockey Town

Zamboni presses a deep kiss
that clean ice smell filling you
hot chocolate sloshing
over the Styrofoam cup
searing your fingertips
erasing the prints
so you're slick and scraped
ready for play.

Expose your five-hole, shock
of possibility. It burns
going down, the liquid in the
toxic cup. In bed, he turns,
a tangle of limbs, and says,

Wouldn't it be funny if…

whiff of his deodorant
dog paw smell of the rink still clinging
to his ungloved hands

summer dark thick as wildberries

shot from the hash marks
blur of puck skittering
over the bad ice
of you

hockey moms hustling up and down
with snacks and signs and crosswords
thinking of their cold boys

the space heater of him
your fingers grazing the crux
surprisingly soft

bouncing off the crossbar
rolling like a meteor
all eyes on its sweet transit
the warmth
on your fingers
as he sighs
unzipping

the mothers screaming
the mothers
and the empty space of the dads
the frozen imprint of them
the Pilsners they'd be holding
their pilot-light eyes
flickering always toward
a bit of violence

his gloves on you
his pads pressing you down
car-trunk leather stench
every particle of him
ice sweat stink
masked in the dark

you've seen him hold it
by the white grid
like a skull
like he's holding his own head

you pass and pass and pass the puck
until you hear the buzzer.

2. CALAMITIES

Dubbed

This summer is for barbecues and lies,
Bon Jovi's voice burns holy as he sings,
I notice that our hands are the same size.

I dream about the ketchup on your fries,
And think of giving you my father's ring,
This summer is for barbecues and lies.

Your hockey glove, the sweet reek of surprise,
Fits. You grin. I forfeit everything.
I notice that our hands are the same size.

I feel your sweat diminish as it dries,
We melt the ice, devouring everything,
This summer is for barbecues and lies.

The mixtape reels and cracks from side to side,
We meet as holy palmers, trembling,
I notice that our hands are the same size.

No record of your dangerous surprise,
We tense ourselves for all that autumn brings;
This summer is for barbecues and lies,
I notice that our hands are the same size.

The Odd

We're pre-drinking at Ron's place on Beach Avenue a condo he affords by renting out the sunroom to exhausted international students. A line of coke shimmers on the countertop. I'm in sweatpants because I don't understand how gay bars work. They have multiple zippers, which makes them, in my eyes, night pants. Ron's place is the staging area for all West End calamities. He readies the shot glasses and vodka sweeps through my gut flora like wildfire. There are two Michaels on the couch, one of them my boyfriend, the other a perilously thin blond who could've stepped off the cover of *XY*. He wears a jade choker and texts faster than anyone you know. I grew up in Chilliwack, where gay people stayed in the basement watching *Four Weddings and a Funeral* on VHS, memorizing the Auden poem John Hannah reads at his Scottish lover's funeral. Now a social worker from St. John's is offering me GHB, which I politely decline. The Michaels are pre-dancing, but one of them doesn't actually dance, it's more like a StairMaster. I've recently watched *Big Eden*, so I dream of returning to my small town and falling in love with a soft-spoken DJ, while my straight high school crush secretly kisses me by a cast iron stove, but the Michaels note that this might be too specific. I do another shot just to fuck with my antidepressant, ignoring the red flags bursting from my body's soil. My doctor says, *There's never been a better cure for anxiety than alcohol,* but it's possible he has a series of pending complaints. I don't know I'm autistic yet, I just think everyone gets tunnel vision at parties and stops talking for days. Ron glides into the kitchen wearing a feather boa. He once claimed his toilet seat was *too small for white people,* but nobody understood. We follow him because he has a golden ticket: a pass for the Odyssey that allows one other person to get in free. It's actually gold, and we've never seen another like it. We walk toward Howe Street and the old house that shelters the club. It already smells like hair gel and 99¢ pizza. The owner's pink Cadillac sleeps by the back door. His name is also Ron, though only Ron has ever laid eyes on him. I know my boyfriend will abandon me as soon as we're inside. He's not cruel, just social, but he also bought me a turtleneck from RW&CO. which made my mom ask, *Does he even know you at all*? When we get in, I head for the patio, where all the flinty twinks are smoking and glaring. One of them registers my night pants, but I'm not such a disaster to hold his attention. I order a triple vodka with cranberry because Margaret Cho says it's good for UTIs. The key is to get drunk enough so I'm loose but not weird, a difficult interval between cheerful and talking incessantly about my old rock tumbler. Someone offers me a joint, maybe blond Michael, or the ghost of autistic queers who knew better. Now the patio tilts to one side. Odysseus lashed himself to the sail, living through siren song, but his real labour was building a bed for Penelope whose roots tied them together. Athena's favourite passes me a vial that smells like burning tires, but I say *No thanks* and then *How's Patroclus?* The answer is *Still dead*, but he breathes it kindly in my ear. Now the boys are climbing into glass cubicles for shower power, soaping their biceps, and Ron steps from the mist. We're on the dance floor, all the Michaels and Rons, every petshop boy, and Paul Monette is whispering something about the last watch of the night, but it's too loud. I wept when I read how his lover's dog Puck would grind against both their knees, how he'd be their widow. Missy Elliott sings "Oops" and we all scream. My hands on Michael's hips, and other Michael's hips, and Ron's soaked t-shirt, and the dead boys, and Patroclus who never grew up to be a doctor, and the doctors who guard the cocktails, and the dogs who will mourn us if we're lucky, and the Odd peels our shirts off, skinning us, until we pulse with blood in the club's hands, the club which will one day be a Nando's PERi-PERi Chicken, a forgetting of glass and steel, one more Vancouver murder, but not yet.

All Asps Forgiven

In college you tasted smoke,
his Middle English mouth. Never,
said Chaucer, was pickerel so wet
as a heart, drowning in love's
brine.

A farm boy
let you skim his sunburn, peeling
dangerously. Furrowing down
his freckled back, the lightest
touch.

A eunuch
from a trashy paperback kept
a snake in their robes, little
curled death, just in case.

Sasha Velour won *Drag Race*, magic's
child. Cracked open their mask and
the world. All wizards are queens
in search of the spell cluster
that will fuse our strength in amber.
All wizards are children, all asps
forgiven.

Feed us stories of scales
and soft killers and cold boys, hatchlings
left by magic to fend. Climb
onto Merlin's bear belly, memory
caterwauling behind, as you
ride out of summer.

South Granville

This poem is actually not about whatever
you're thinking, but rather the brush of
fingertips on an accent wall, snick of chrome
on skin, sadness that escapes an uncorked
bottle. We talk about Plato because we're
those people, I'm still in grad school, you've
survived a philosophy degree. I love that
moment in the *Symposium* where Alcibiades
crashes the party, drunk and half-naked, then
calls out Socrates: *He's nothing but a cheap
satyr toy with no centre.* In his defence,
I've also been uncomfortable at sleepovers.
I can't remember everything we said, just
the pilled surface of your fleece jacket,
like an old cat's fur, and the way you leaned
imperceptibly closer. Your occasional laugh
cracking a crème brûlée to reveal a sea of
gold, the way Socrates describes goodness as
an even wave swallowing us all. This poem
isn't about Socrates either, though he clings
to its edge, not wanting to miss out. We meet
for a second date at your place in South
Granville, where I could never afford to live.
White women walk French bulldogs on their
way to the opera. I linger at Pottery Barn,
gazing at a leather chair that costs more than
my salary for a four-month teaching contract.
I touch it, because why not? Future me will

hear the character Freckle say, *Sometimes*
things that are expensive are worse.
But I don't know that yet. I walk to your
townhouse (a house in town, an *entire*
house) and there's a little gate, useless but
still pointed in its message. You let me in.
The pasta you're making smells clean, like
every burnished surface. I stare at the glass
stovetop, which reminds me of this family
I babysat for in the nineties. How I'd marvel
at their burners, red eyes, winking on to
cook the Kraft dinner I'd brought from home.
I'd phone my friend, who was busy
killing the queen in her fantasy novel,
and we'd laugh over the latest episode of
Buffy the Vampire Slayer, the one where
Willow accidentally scans a demon into
the library's PC. But I don't write anymore,
I just order interlibrary loans and go on
dates where guys say *Don't touch my feet*
or *Can my cats watch?* The wine is a season
giving way, and I stare at your mouth as you
describe the job I can't remember. I work
until another laugh rises out of you, clear
as the creaky bucket in *The Little Prince*,
and now it's warm and our shy asteroids drift
closer still. You lead me upstairs and I see
a glimpse of your bedroom—white duvet,
clothes on the floor a scattering of tasteful
leaves—before we land on the couch, watching

TV, but nothing specific, until we collapse
into each other, a house giving way to the
fault in its basement. A weather report
makes you chuckle and your breath stirs the
hairs on my neck. We're a living chesterfield,
one of my favourite words, your fingers gliding
down my arm, the Brillo pad of your thumb
polishing me. It's better that we can't see
each other, because my face is doing a thing
and if I turn around I don't know what I'll
see, what I'll give away. How long do we
stay like this? I know the light changes. I
feel the heat click on, the house wanting to
comfort us. You walk me to the door and
we all know what happens next. I incline
towards you. Our lips touch, but when I pull
away the look on your face is astonishing.
Like you've reached for a last step but found
winter instead. Some primordial recalibration.
I think of it on the way home, as the cable
bus sparks across the bridge. I think of it
in the silence that honeys between us, day
after day. Your face will always be my
wildest grammar failure, the shocked moment
when you mean to say *I had a nice night*,
but *night* becomes the memory of seeing your
teenage crush slip from his sleeping bag
to open the window, a flash of hip in the
dark, your mouth going dry, before you
even understood what wine
could taste like.

Tenderfoot

They refuse to leave
in the end
the pigeons
their tender feet
clutching at the nails
on our sill
watching us
all summer.

The lais
of Marie de France
slip from nerveless fingers
as I'm lapped
by Toronto's hot
tongue. In Montevideo,
you say, a raw egg
boils on your skin
surrendering
gold.

I'm awful
at conjugations. I ask
why every word
lays as it does.

Chiquito, you beg,
stop playing
that fucking
Shakira song.

It's the one
where she's trapped
under the pavement
and wanting
to go
even deeper.

I burn
with jealousy
over your trilingual friends
and the boy
who rubs your shoulders
a bit too often.

When I tell you
about the job offer
in Saskatchewan
you push me
like a bumper car
crying
as our verb
slips its track.

The night before we fly,
I drink tequila like
I'm on a mission. A cat
named Samson bites my face
but I forgive him.

The prairies
are golden squares
we circle, dehydrated,
afraid. Your hand
on my knee. I remember

the commotion
when you dragged our mattress
across the parquet floor
in the burning sun
que sueñes
con los angelitos
and we slept
filthy-footed angels
thatched by light
the rustling wings
the edges so near.

Winter Skips

We're listening to *Winter*
by Tori Amos, our Discmans
burning our laps, as the piano solo
unbolts us. You pass me a note
that's just the number of times
you've heard it today: *21*.

We get caught staring
at the Leonardo DiCaprio poster.
We're only letting ourselves
go fuzzy for a moment. Skipping
forward because we think
that's the good part.

You're typing with an Australian guy
on IRC. You smile imperceptibly
when he sends you files. I'm jealous
of your internet package:
my modem a screaming brick
with ideas of its own.

We stage a scene from *Sailor Moon*
where Tuxedo Mask is stalked,
tenderly, by a gay alien. We use
flour to dye our hair,
making pancakes in the shower.

Our manuscripts are crammed
into sawtooth binders. You read me
a death, a birth, over the phone
until I can't feel my cheek.

We're unknown and furious
in hidden classrooms, plotting
while everyone fails to play Magic:
The Gathering, or maybe just me. Cards
in boxes like organ slices, red, blue,
black. The spell that always wins
if you're cruel enough to cast it.

In the end, the only move I make
on the boy I love unspeakably
is to destroy his coffee maker.
Flooding the kitchen, twisting
in panic as he laughs, then hoses it off
in the yard like a dog's empty cage.
You're lucky, he says,
that we love you.

The Tribble

I approach the panel. Your blazer makes
my eyes wend. Are you there, Catullus?
I need to borrow the spindles of fate.

You lift the lid. The tribble is old,
practically coming undone.

I catch archive fever.

Your dog tackles me like Hobbes
when I open a door. A scoop of
wet food pacifies her. Beards tickle
while she dreams under the afghan.

Winter licks the doorstop as
Obama makes his entrance.
We fall off the chesterfield,
tangled in a string of lights.

My argument won't coalesce.
I don't know what to say about
winged ones guarding his funeral.
Those archons in the margins.

We watch reruns of *House*, avoiding
the garrulous lobby where battered
hopefuls crisp in a cast-iron pan.

Shadows make trouble.
Desires abrade the duotang.
The wharf is like Coal Harbour in
Vancouver, jewelled by gulls.

Streetcars bump at salient angles.
The lever sings. My geometry is
weak, but our hands solve for Y.

At the airport, I declare a finger puppet,
a mercy letter, snow-streaked clay,
some of the dog's orange frass. Nothing
I can't carry on.

Draft Poems

A poem about the boy who worked
at a deli counter. He'd slice pastrami
during the day and drive an hour
to visit you at night, slipping
through the basement door
like a burglar, touching you with
fingers so close to the blade.

A poem about the nineties café
that sold endless varieties of cheese
cake, all of which, at varying times,
made you shit yourself on first dates,
though the bathroom always
smelled like cinnamon.

A poem about the time you melted
down in sixth grade, and the teacher
stood in the hallway as you shook
silently, your mullet, your off-
brand shoes, the shirt that said *not
playing with a full duck*, and you
weren't, anyone could see that.

A poem about the nurse who gave you
tea then led you to a bedroom filled
with mirrors, and you both snorted,
oracular pigs tangled in blankets,
bellies pressed together, a low-speed
chase that ended with a tongue
untying a gracious knot.

A poem about the crucifix hanging
in the bedroom of St. Paul's hospital
where you shivered with sepsis,
pissing into a bucket that measured
fluid like a toddler learning to hit
the bull's eye, Christ shrugging on his
rood as if to remind you that bodies
are mostly water and emptiness.

A poem about the time we skipped
karaoke to smoke stems on the tiny
glass patio, the impossible condo,
watching the slick tour buses
beach themselves on Robson,
your laugh unravelling me, gathering
smoke in the pipe's clay heart.

A poem about your plasma globe in
the old house in East Van with the
turret, the shut-in neighbour, crows
watching us lie on the floor while
we listened to Radiohead, and you
asking, *Are we stereotypes?*

A poem about never looking people
in the eye, where each line defers the
subject, like that nineties screen saver
where the glowing square cannot,
in spite of its best intentions, quite
reach the corner, though we live
in reckless hope.

It's Funny

I used to say *it's funny* whenever
I wanted to introduce an obscurity,
an obsession, a cat fact, a geode,
a ribbon of wild speculation,
until an ex told me to stop because
preserved bog bodies and imperial
Roman hairstyles aren't technically
hilarious, more like the winter-
licked stones that some penguins
carry to show one another:
Have you seen my wares?

Your teenager wakes you at 4 a.m.
to show you a boss battle. Minutes
ago, they shouldered the penguin
backpack full of plumes and canopic
jars and the memory of a zoetrope
spinning first shadow then light,
then again. Seconds ago, we were
little meteors. We carried our own
sweet paraphernalia. We drank from
the hose. A dog coughed on our
bare feet. We stole a piece of salt-
water taffy then returned it, our
criminal career over before it began.

After two radlers, I admit, *If you*
asked me to marry you, I'd probably
say yes. I've managed to sunburn
a single knee and later I'll destroy
the bathroom as the cat waits
by the door wondering what
strange closet I've disappeared in.

It's funny: a boy once vowed
revenge on me in the eighth grade.
I'd ruined his life a few years
earlier, surprising even myself.

Like Barbie, I'm thinking more
about death and what it means
to die well and alone in a world
on fire. I imagine a pyre on a
lava flow. Nurses will sometimes
make false hands out of water
balloons, so we have some warmth
to hold onto. I think of the restlessness
that precedes death, and what rumination
might lead me from my pallet
into the burning hallway. I try to
see what I'm seeing—but maybe
it's something that hasn't been
invented yet, or something
too old and fragile to explain.

It's funny: I live with the dread
of a white-tailed jackrabbit skittering
across an open plain of hostilities.

You know when you're writing a poem
and it suddenly sees you? One sodium
light reaching from far away, or perhaps
closer than you'd realized? It gets longer
and longer because it wants to keep living,
and isn't that relatable?

It's funny: we're at the campus
gathering, and wind is blowing
the president's speech away.
I steal a gluten-free bun by accident,
hiding it in my bag like a condom.
Wasps are drawn to our wild hair,
streaming out like dendrite
branches. Your youngest chose
the camp option described as sports
plus sports. Your eldest is coding
in a cool, dark place. It's funny, but

I can see the world they're building,
fact by sly fact, how everything
will bloom where it lies.

The Most Immersive Experience

There's an error with the Van Gogh
exhibit and in place of *Starry Night*,
a screen at our feet says *auto*
searching. I have food poisoning
from chicken fingers I ate
in Weyburn. You made us stop
at the pub because it sounded
like a gay bar in Vancouver. I asked
for a matchbook, and the server
looked at me oddly as if I'd un-
seamed her memory. The next two days
are a lens flare. I dream of Indiana Jones
foiling a Nazi time-travel plot,
which actually happens at the drive-in,
shivering, your hand in mine, his thumb
brushing the face of Archimedes.
You become a human heating pad,
covering every inch of me.

Van Gogh looms, an event
horizon where I hopefully
won't vomit on your sister.
I nap in your bed while you
attack giant bugs in an old game.
Your hot air balloon won't work,
and this is the only way to grow
in a world of dragons. I hear
Athena, lend me your power
muffled by the pillow as
your cat settles nearby,
drawn to my radioactivity.

If she had wings, you say,
nothing would be safe.
But now Van Gogh is pouring
sadness into cobalt fire
in spite of the network
connectivity problem. His digital bio
includes a letter to Theo
where he writes of being
an outcast. *I will show everyone*
what is in the heart of a nobody.

A Don McLean song filters through
the sound system and I feel myself,
awfully, start to cry as I think about
Vincent's mental supernova, how
he painted stars through the barred
window of the sanitarium, though
maybe it's just the poison slowly
leaving me. Your sister's friend
tells stories at dinner, mostly
involving nudity, as I eat individual
grains of rice. I'm asked, unironically,
if I enjoy ice fishing, and I can't look
at you, because I know your grin
will break me into painful laughter.
You lead me back to your place, one step
at a time, Athena's power lifting us up
the stairs, but it's your hand on my back,
it's your arms circling me as the stars
go offline, even in front of your
brother-in-law, your voice in my ear:
Just don't look at the floor.

3. EPISODES

Speech Delay

Six years before you arrive at words, instead
you point and laugh, your face often trembling
between intensities, until the morning you spill
every sentence in your oatmeal like wild honey.

You point and laugh, your face often trembling
in the mirror as you try on different smiles,
pulling expressions from the hidden fascia,
then Windex the glass and wipe away each line.

In the mirror as you try on different smiles
the bright outside works your blown glass true
no words in the glory hole, only trembling
sweetbitter plasma, the hiss of understanding.

The bright outside works your blown glass true
but a fourth state of matter between intensities
tries you on, mirror of your motion, wild honey
before you arrive at words, or waves, or years.

Spidey Sense

At the centre for re-
alignment, I read pamphlets
on how to be socially appropriate.
I tell a story about
Monopoly pieces and empathy.

High-functioning shit-show.
Low-needs.
Lo-fi.
Masking queen.

I walk home through prairie
fire with a muddy diagnosis.
Identity buried in paperwork.

A shiver passes through me
like that eighties movie
where the immortal highlanders
smell each other, hackles raised

and there you are
in front
of the stained-glass repair shop.

We hold our precious cargo,
the years of hiding, only to
flare out now. Shake our frames
in the winter sun. *I know*
you. We met at a bonfire
fuelled by diagnostic manuals.

We cross to the path
of leaves, two cracks in the air.

Shy against so much light.

Tism

TikTok is full of Homeric epithets like
bi wife energy, and the latest is something
called *tism rizz*, which refers to a curious
charm possessed by autistic people, a kind
of mental catnip that makes us irresistible
as partners. We're so quirky and fun, like
Popples from the eighties who would curl
into a ball at parties. We skate across
social conventions with our manic pixie
dream brains and isn't that just so fucking
cute? How we don't get any supports?
How we're often melting down in the
frozen food aisle because they won't
stop playing "Backstreet's Back" and all
we want is a bag of non-artisanal
perogies to eat in silence? And isn't
it precious how we can be fired for
being difficult whenever we question
rules based on hierarchy and white
supremacy? And isn't it sexy how
I close my office door and melt down
after every department meeting because
I can't still my body for two hours,
can't listen to one more person defend
a vampiric university that grinds up
students and instructors while deans
promote abusers then show up to
protests and the president takes credit

for the diversity policy we spent three
years fighting for, and isn't it hot when
I ask you to squeeze me as tight as you
can while I'm having a panic attack,
like that machine Temple Grandin invented
to comfort cows? But you do. You rub
my arms up and down. You call me a
burrowing owl as I nose my way into
all your corners. Was it my rizz that
attracted you? I've never felt charming,
though people call me that. Every ex
has frowned at me, the way you'd perceive
a maple bug who appears in the middle
of winter. *Why? How?* Because we
live in the motherfucking walls, making
our nests. We sun ourselves on social
porches, on the shores of loud parties,
waiting for the moment to unveil our
magnificent rizz. And if you reach
for us in violence, we'll emit a toxin
that summons armies, adorable clouds
of hunger and sleeplessness and
special knowledge and missed cues
and wrong touches and literal answers
and sketchy eye contact and stripped
nerves and nothing will hold us back,
nothing except for your hands rubbing
up and down my arms, your smile
when you say *I'll be your chew toy,*
and I chew, I do.

Woof

Scruff is an app
for people
who think
they're better than Grindr.

A *woof* says you're cute
but not enough to message.

Living with dogs, I know
that a woof can mean
danger
love
hunger
my toy
my bed
my precious stick.

The bars are always
baffling and dark. I order
chicken fingers and keep
my autistic paws quiet

under the table.

I didn't used to talk. I learned
by Duolingo. You'll hear
a faint accent.

The guy tells me about
the time he passed out in a bathtub
the scar on his wrist
a demure bite. He works
for a hockey team whose mascot
is endangered. He's everyone
I've ever listened to
in a maze of pint glasses
and furious eyes.

Our tails could make
a love knot, but in
the end, I don't
woof.

When I get home
the husky forms
an ivory comma:
we wait
for her brother to explode
down the stairs
on hot golden springs.

How many times
have I pulled something
from your jaws
that startled me?

Pressed by warm fur, I open
the app. A *woof.* A night
stretching perfectly blank.

Do dogs tire of barking?
Never. We sing
from deep in our throats
all the way down
to the joy box. We give
everything away.

Pronoun Policy

My province is forcing trans kids
to come out to their families because
parents have rights too, even though
they don't, not actually, and the wrap-
around supports promised by the
government amount to nothing but
the rage of Christian dads, being
kicked out and told you aren't
who you are, while Scott Moe
does his best to override the Charter,
and Steve Balog keeps filing FOI
requests to learn more about how
the premier killed his mother in
a car accident, perhaps still feeling
the pain of those broken ribs, crush
of glass, Moe skating away with no
charges, his giant belt buckle a jet
pack rocketing him towards the
legislature where one day, he'll
invoke the notwithstanding clause
to implode the lives of trans kids
because he's scared of losing his
voter base to a party demanding
justice for white gun-owners, and
as my co-worker's kid climbs a
tree to better hear their speech
about being a trans parent, I see
their fingers grip the branches,

while straight pride flags droop
like funereal gloves behind
the barricade, and I steal the little
flag from my living room to wave
like someone with absolutely no
pattern recognition, but when I
was a trans kid I wanted to be a
falcon, a nameless sorceress,
a collection of garlands, David
Bowie's feather cloak from
Labyrinth, a strange light moving
over the face of Cultus Lake
as I pushed against the gravity
of water with my cupped hand,
again and again, how it felt like
a word in my palm, and I wanted
nothing more than to dissolve into
the transporter buffer on *Star Trek*,
just a dangerous glass of electrified
ginger ale fizzing between neutral
zones, and all those years later, drunk
in the Bay change room, asking *What
should I do with these tassels?* and
you said *Whatever you want*, so I
wrapped them around me, and it
never stopped, the lick of fear when
I'd wear a skirt to class, bare arms
with their fading tattoos, never
expecting to play an archangel in

Paradise Lost, sweating in the hot
theatre with administrators frowning
at my outfit, or was that just my
paranoia of never feeling trans enough
while watching the cis asteroid field
pass me by in my shuttle craft, no
impulse control, just drifting, and
Scott Moe would have run me over
if he'd known me then, all the good
believers who just can't understand
pronouns when G-d said *I am what*
I am what I was what I will be, and
we chant *Kyrie eleison* and we chant
Shame! and my boyfriend came out
late because his whole town told him
being queer was a sin, and a sin is
a word with an unclear etymology,
it means painful knowledge, the right
kind of flaw, and I need to tell you,
please listen, there's no heaven or
hell, only this bewildering dancefloor,
Middle-earth that fucks with you
but sometimes touches your cheek,
and I know your name,
I do, I'll say it
with you, I'll
say it, I'll
say it.

Marlena Is Once Again Possessed

Marlena is once again possessed
by the devil on *Days of Our Lives*
and only John Black, her ex-
mercenary lover, can save her.

I used to cut class to watch her
levitate, her cheap yellow contacts
peeling back my skin. She saw
everything: my lies, my frailty,
the loves I underfed in secret.

All the way from Salem, the devil
rose from her floral bedspread
to measure my soul against a
synthetic feather. That town
where you might be twinned,
resurrected, devoured.

I knew all the made-up towns ruled
by scandal. Port Charles with its
hospital corridors. Genoa City
where Nikki wept into her car-
phone on *The Young and the*
Restless, trapped by a blizzard
and her love for Victor.

All we had was a drive-thru
corn barn, and the hope that
it wouldn't die by lightning—
so far from *Santa Barbara,*
where Sawyer boxed shirtless
and made me twist my crucifix.

We still watch *Y&R,* now mostly
about corporate takeovers
and the considerable paperwork
of Jabot Cosmetics. The new romantic
frontier: sexy companies dragging
tongues over each other.

My mom snorts to discover
that Marlena is still possessed
after all these years. *It was stupid
the first time around.*

But Mom, this is all there is.
Sinister bedrooms and parking garages,
cafes and promenades
and lounges where we engineer
our little catastrophes.

Brad rising wet from Lauren's pool,
his speedo a black hole sucking in
small-town queers, our little lights
crashing into his v-cut before
that was a word, because it's 1987
and all we have is hunger,
and the jaws of AIDS
coming for all of us, but how

astonishing to stand for a moment
in Brad's heat, to pry the cordless
phone from his hand, the antenna
squealing, his straight unscarred body
and Lauren touching her mouth in
bewilderment as we lean forward,
grazing his jaw, to whisper the names
of our dead, until he falls to his knees,
possessed by an unstoppable force.

Leaving the Shire

Your dog's fur collects
in the empty crate
along with my cat's ghost
and autumn
as we slip from
our separate coordinates.

The hotel knows itself:
haunted blue carpets,
decaying glamour.
I step from the shower
and you ask where I went
like the bathroom
is a wormhole.

In the famous bookstore
I sneak a glance
at your spine: a novel
where boys kiss on prom night
and no one's scared
no one's dead
the waffle house keeps them all
under its heat lamp,
queer goslings.

Fireworks crackle
along the dark Willamette
green waves
breaking over us.
I'm a gobsmacked hobbit
veiled in artificial light,
your hand nervous in mine.
Candy floss tall as French wigs
webbing us together.

We nearly trip
over fossilized tramlines,
laughing. We push
the beds together
and I glance at the door
between rooms:
sealed Narnian chamber
still breathing.

You undress
my American side:
Jersey roots, my grandfather's
stern neurotype, my dad stoned
and listening to Steely Dan
in Kendall Park.

I'm too careful. I never know
if you're really here. You slide
down your boxers and smirk.
The familiar puzzle
in my hand, the fit of us.

In the morning you hunt
Pokémon while I check in early
for this familiar ache—
a/c raising gooseflesh
my nose in your crook
trying to save
that clean cat smell.

The Repair Shop

After my mother's heart
attack, we watch a show
where all manner of broken
things receive care
under a thatched roof.

A twisted Dalek slurs
as men whisper carefully
over its pebbled body.

It belonged to a boy
with no friends
who carried it up
imagined ice floes
touching the little
homicidal plungers
for luck.

When her heart was
outside her body, hands
fluttered over all
that she was, coaxing
music back to the
atrial halls, from the
door where it had
nearly fled.

We all fail in drawers
and dark basements
pins worn down
until someone gathers us
turns on the light
and goes to work.

When she called me in
the deep dale of night
on the way to surgery
did I taste the icing
she once ate between
graham crackers
as a child?

Did I feel the baton
dance from her hand
fibrillating
frozen in the sky's
antechamber, the static,
her voice climbing up
that same glacier
under the Dalek's curious eye?

I've never wished
to be fixed
but wouldn't say no
to the kiss
of a delicate weld.

For every lost key
in the master's bowl
there is a startled lock.

For first and final loves,
a solvent. For regret,
a clever tool. For the broken
gnome, an understated
new face.

There's a trick to unbreak
every heart, only learned
by touching *here* and *here*
and *here.*

4. TRANSITS

Glass Crack Time Machine

I turn away from the window, anticipating a blow.
I thought I'd find myself

an old woman by now, travelling so light in time.
But I haven't gotten far at all.

– Brenda Shaughnessy, "I Have a Time Machine"

Your six-year-old had a time machine hidden
in the pocked surface of the beige car's wind-
shield, a long scar that puckered past and
future as we bumped along the lunar surface
of Saskatchewan roads. Remember when we
lost ourselves on the way to the Sears outlet
in search of a bed I could live with, driving
deeper through gold and stone, until the
graveyard rose up to meet us? The mourners
a seam along burnt grass. You asked, *Should*
we apologize? But now the car wash nudges
us forward year by year, and your youngest
grins at the light show, telling me that apple-
green is the finest colour. I turn away from
the window, anticipating a blow.

There's a laptop locked in the amber of '97,
watching over my adolescent bedroom with
frozen dignity. A few old emails ghost around
Eudora, including a response to a personal ad:
I guess I've written a novel again. Why did I

always apologize for all those hot keys when
text was my first language? She forgets
how to reach the internet, but sometimes I
unsnarl her heavy cord, plug her in, and feel
the old codes pulling me back to my Christian
town where it was fine to be queer and silent
as long as you went to youth group. That time
you took a hairpin turn in your dad's Aerostar,
hurling me through space, and I bent around
the rod of the fake tree, ultimately fine, though
I thought I'd find myself.

Now we're moving faster. The grad school
era, when we learned to drink and sit on the
white pine floors of professorial homes, letting
the wine draw us forward, then back. All the
footnotes and the bus rides at dawn, smell of
sour coffee on anxious lips, the skinny boys
with Marxist cowlicks who set fire to Norton
anthologies, dancing around the wastebasket
until security arrived. We're in the old room
again, staring out the porthole. Where have
all the Magic cards gone? A squirrel stole
them to feather his den, but broke both legs.
How far he must have pushed himself, until
he arced like snow from the exhausted branch.
I thought I'd be an old woman by now,
travelling so light in time.

This memory card has one last open door,
which caves to my touch. I pilot us back
to your town, where a sinister Santa towers
over the freeway entrance. The grid roads
lead us to your dad's forage land where
everything is sunburnt pink. GPS doesn't
exist yet. Just arrow sights on old tractors
and your nineties laser portrait. The timing
belt is worn to grey, but there's just enough
light to see you, a field shadow, holding
your grandmother's camera. I'm Marty
McFly, dim in the wheat. Sound of pulses
dancing in the lentil factory so close. You take
my picture, but it's too late, I'm already kissing
you and it's funny, I thought the telephone
poles moved so swiftly beyond the glass,
but I haven't gotten far at all.

Undo List

didn't kiss
in the parklet

didn't chase you
down the jetway

didn't reach
across choking summer
body fear sharper
than cow shit
until our seams
untouched

didn't play
Mama Cass
in brushfire ruins

didn't fit
your prom dress

didn't have a brilliant
difficult kid
in Montreal didn't but

almost

and that rogue passenger
didn't call me by name
and say *If you have a*
child you should lift
it and

I didn't explain

this is no stranger's moon
no unceded meteor

but all for you
even my ache
the incomplete arc of us
under light travelling
at impossible speeds.

Checkup

A friend touches my shoulder
briefly
and I realize
only nurses
have touched me
for six months.

His fingers
dance along the fault
in our bodies.

I've got a closet full
of gauze
and no dinner dates.
Smoke gathers around
St. Paul's Hospital. The sun
a bleary eye.

I ask my therapist
about bubble sex.
I dream of you
touching a plant
you brought back to life.

Cruising involves
averted eyes. We turn delicately
from each other, as if from
a prairie wind. I feel a small
meteor in my gut
when someone beautiful
keeps their distance.

My mom sends cookies
as attachments. The cinnamon smell
takes us back to Bloomsbury.
Warm in our hands
as we stare at the British Library.
In a moment, we'll touch
the earth-locked book
of leech remedies,
ghostly crumbs on our fingers.

Mouthful

You wake up
with a mouth
full of night no

blood

life is a crime scene
in your sink.

The alarm cackles
in the ER bathroom
as you spit
clot after clot
and a guard calls:

You need to activate
the motion sensor.
Do a jumping jack.

After electrocuting
your gums, the doctor
applies surgical foam,

This stuff costs
$400 a package.

You almost say
Broken system huh
but it's so late
and you can't lecture
this tired man
wearing a mask
with dancing tomatoes.

You measure time
by
dripping

until finally
this staunched body
leads you
down Davie Street
in unexpected light
and you see
nerves of nightshade
stretched across a wall
their mouths full
of swollen gold.

Remember your lips
buzzing from that first
kiss. Filled with another
boy's heat. Red mouth
as if you'd been
smacked.

The words that knot
your tongue. *Spit*
it out. Ah! To gleek
every unsaid thing
onto the astonished floor
like a wet moth.

Take yourself home
and see
cast off in haste
on the lintel
a bloody print
your own scattered petal
indelible.

How to Stay Gay in Quarantine

Every walk a lesson
in desire. Others like you
move between houses with
better gardens.

You catch sight of them,
in fence slats and the oracle
of fallen branches. You all
peregrinate in your best
feathered memories.

Ramble with a queer friend
to the pointless bridge where pelicans
once astonished you. Laugh and
sweat over your profiles. Small-
town quarks in parallel dances.

Try a social-distance date where
instead of kissing, you analyze
a telenovela. If he also loves
the honeyed pauses
of Paulina de la Mora, then

you'd better not _____ by the bleachers.

Zoom with friends who are
forgetting how to be queer. Un-
washed, buffered, breaking. Kiss
good night but stay online
to hear the little snores.

Like the monk Alcuin, write
to ask for your book back,
then accidentally
declare your love to every ex
in the postscript.

Seethe over the flaws
of *Drag Race*. Hear the echo
of ancestors whose old skirts
trailed across unsanitary lanes.

You are also a molly. Also
Princess Seraphina, put on trial
in 1732. Your neighbour, the
washerwoman, defends you
for stealing back your shoes.

I see you at Cabela's, looking confused.

I see you on grid roads. In bookstores,
touching the pages. Remembering
patios in Montreal
where our worlds tilted like the apartment floor.

Live-stream old relationships to your head.
The guy who said *Don't touch my feet.*
The pilot you waltzed with. The pen pal
from Vigo you met years later, floating
in the Teleférico above the cruising park.

I kept it, he said, referring to the sun
you'd mailed him when you were both
fifteen, *until all the rays broke off.*

Tremors

You twitch in your sleep
hands fluttering over me
like some ghost in you
wants to raise a song
from my skin. I let you
play all my broken keys
this unconscious adagio
you won't remember.

I count between tremors,
as your little lightning
circles us in bed. You sink
fathoms and I wonder,
amid flowering kelp, if
you see your father in
a coral cap, my aunt's
impossible beehive.

Does this greening river
connect us both? What
do they say in their
pearled silence? Catch
them if you can, love
a wriggling nightcrawler
as bait. Wrap them in
sheets that smell of us.

This is the only way
to speak with the dead:
carefully, underwater,
in shutter clicks. Your hand
startles itself against
my wrist. You feather
awake, but something
blue between us

keeps swimming.

Hairball

Sometimes I still hear my cat throwing
up, that wet sound of pulling something
deep from within. Haven't we all dredged
the dark lakes of our bodies in search of
a memory to lay upon the hardwood? She
grew louder with age until she would cry
in the blue hour of the night, lost in our
studio apartment. Sometimes I wake and
don't recognize the curtains, the light,
the outline I've traced in my own bed.

In the final years, she would eat only
the fishiest of sauces, laced with pill
powder that made her grimace with a
look of betrayal. She slept on our old
CD changer, unbothered by the Boney M.
record spinning so close. It was heat
that she searched for, curling into the
corners of our bodies, the soft parts,
forming a black comma beneath the
duvet that remembered other cats.

In the end she stopped drinking
and looked like a coat tossed
carelessly on the couch. The vet techs
kept apologizing. *We don't normally need*
this much sedation. But we smiled, because
it was her prerogative to be difficult on
this very last day. She looked at me, aware
and fighting the drugs. I said *Okay, okay,*
watching death travel down the catheter,

wondering if I would be so perfectly awake.

My Boyfriend Names Every Bond Movie Chronologically

In bed, I ask the most important question:
Can Dr. No's mechanical hands hold on
tenderly? There's a moment where Bond
imagines himself as a woman in the dark
slash of mirror. I imagine myself as
various German castles I'd like to visit,
fingers tracing my *Wassergraben*, and
their little ducks. Colonel Klebb skims the
skirt of her Russian operative. Lesbians
wear envenomed shoes. We laugh as
Bond hops around in the final scene,
trying to avoid the prick. Villains earn
gold signet rings, and I'd join SPECTRE
for fashion. My boyfriend maps Granville
Island Market like Q studying the Aston
Martin's specs. *Choose the first thing
your heart desires.* We invent a cat-themed
series of Bond films: *Tabbies Are Forever,
Gold Toe Beans, Her Majesty's Secret
Purr-Fest.* The mint doughnut tastes
like another life, where I stayed in this
impossible city. He grew up in a town
where adults crossed to the other side of
the street when they saw him, a twelve-
year-old, because he didn't attend the right
Christian school. I grew up wanting to be
one of the queen's beautiful devices,

a firing pin, sly tracker in some
finer shoe. It took twenty years to score an
invite to this festival, and now I'm crying
in boutique sheets, pain sharp as the
diamond that keeps Shirley Bassey warm,
rain snaking against the useless patio, and
he says *Hold on to me, I'm your support
bear*. Did Q do this for Bond? When
the space between live and let die grew
thin, did he gather 007 in the compass
of his arms? Hush him in the backseat of
the flying car? Scaramanga would make
the perfect cat villain, since he already has
too many nipples. In the haunted green room,
poets joke about Sor Juana and how she felt
like an emotional hedgehog. Stage lights
pool around my divorced parents in the
front row. He sits between them, a spy
who loves me, as a poet rakes the moon,
praising libraries and Hypatia, whose eyes
saw a perfect golden grid before she was
martyred, and did Synesius inhale the scent
of her letters as I snuffle the clean flush of his
two-in-one? In another life, Pussy Galore
leaves her queer air circus to run the Great
Library of Alexandria, and someone tells my
boyfriend, at twelve, that kissing a boy will
invite neither miracle nor disaster, simply an
unexpected view, like pulling down the
shade to see mountains. Daylights confuse

our light meters, but I keep taking the same
photo of him, legs splayed on the couch,
silvered laugh, shadows intact, and I wish
our government didn't have a licence to
kill trans kids, but how can I leave this bright
horizon? The cat and the chaise and most
of my poems are here. Do spies have nine lives,
like queers who survive the prairies? A world
can be enough if you sweet-talk the celestial
thermostat. My boyfriend calls chickpea fries
bullshit and I agree, but things can also be
other, miracles reversed, day another die,
another roll for damage, and sometimes free
nuts in the breakout room. Bond bets all
at the quantum casino as Q waits for him,
barefoot, in a sealed, painless hotel room,
wearing race-car PJs, the bed covered in
gorgeous schematics, and every breath
in the hallway makes him shiver. *Sky Paws.*
You Only Meow Twice. One day our cat
will be a spectre haunting the couch divot,
but now my boyfriend, grinning as we
prepare our descent, limbs tangled to spite
the Sask Party, mouth close to my ear,
crumbs from the WestJet biscuit ghosting
his fingers, having trained so long for
this mission, grain truck to spaceship,
ecstatic, sings the last perfect detail:
We have no time to die.

ACKNOWLEDGEMENTS

[illegible]

[illegible]

ACKNOWLEDGEMENTS

Thanks to my mother who remembers the dramatic poem about time and space I wrote when I was twelve and always reminds me of it. And thanks to my father for setting an example of leaving in the middle of parties. And thanks to Kathleen Wall, Michael Trussler, and Melanie Schnell for their valuable insight on draft poems. And thanks to Medrie Purdham for understanding the difficulty of time machine maintenance. And thanks to D for reading and being in some of these poems. And thanks to Sam for texting to notify me that we exist. And thanks to Bea for a lifelong exchange of vibrant postcards. And thanks to June for the penguins and friendly ghosts. And thanks to M for doing the time warp. And thanks to RJ for showing us Nico's precious nose. And thanks to Child for looking skeptical on the cover. And thanks to Courtney Bates-Hardy and Tea Gerbeza for their beautiful and true work. And thanks to John Loeppky for reminding me to be scrappy. And thanks to all my creative writing students for producing whole galaxies under pressure. And thanks to my bookshelves for their emotional labor. And thanks to the ones we mourn and the ones we fight alongside. And thanks to my body and mind for this moment and the next.

Poems from this collection previously appeared in the */tƐmz/ Review*, the *Malahat Review*, *Impossible Archetype*, *Ghost City Review*, the *Ex-Puritan*, *Eunoia Review* and *CV2*.

ABOUT THE AUTHOR

Photo credit: Devin Wilger

Jes Battis is from Chilliwack, B.C. (Stó: lō territory) and currently lives in Regina, Saskatchewan (Treaty Four). They teach creative writing, literature, and trans and queer studies. They've published work previously in the *Capilano Review*, the *Ex-Puritan*, the *Malahat Review* and *poetry is dead*, as well as the *Los Angeles Review of Books* and *Strange Horizons*. They're a Gemini who has learned to hate parties a bit less over the years. Their spiritual parents are Odo from *Deep Space Nine* and the sorceress from *Masters of the Universe*. Their fiction has been included in *Canada Reads* and shortlisted for the Sunburst Award. They are haunted by several cats.